Yellow Umbrella Books are published by Capstone Press
151 Good Counsel Drive, P.O. Box 669, Mankato, Minnesota 56002
www.capstonepress.com

Library of Congress Cataloging-in-Publication Data
Trumbauer, Lisa, 1963–
   Let's graph / by Lisa Trumbauer.
   p. cm.
   Summary: Simple text and photographs introduce the concept of graphing and
present examples of two different kinds of graphs.
   ISBN 0-7368-2932-6 (hardcover)—ISBN 0-7368-2891-5 (softcover)
   1. Graphic methods—Juvenile literature. [1. Graphic methods.] I. Title.
QA90.T785 2004
518'.23-dc2z   2003012330

Editorial Credits

Editorial Director: Mary Lindeen
Editor: Jennifer VanVoorst
Photo Researcher: Wanda Winch
Developer: Raindrop Publishing

Photo Credits

Cover: Tom and DeeAnn McCarthy/Corbis; Page 2: Photo courtesy of Lammersville
School, Tracy, CA; Page 3: Annie Griffiths Belt/Corbis; Page 4: Ryan McVay/Photodisc;
Page 5: Corel; Page 6: Comstock; Page 7: Comstock; Pages 8–9: Corel (left), Comstock
(middle, right); Page 10: Ryan McVay/Photodisc; Pages 11–13: Comstock (top left, top
right), Corel (bottom left); Page 14: Stockbyte; Page 15: George Disario/Corbis; Page
16: Russell Burden/Index Stock Imagery

1 2 3 4 5 6 09 08 07 06 05 04

Let's Graph

by Lisa Trumbauer

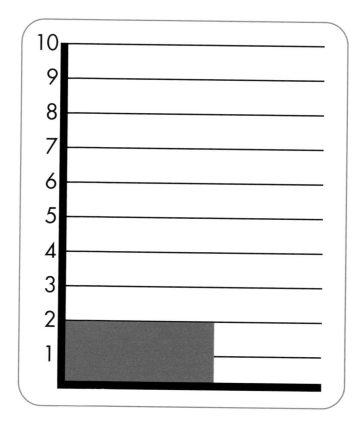

Consultants: David Olson, Director of Undergraduate Studies, and Tamara Olson, PhD, Associate Professor, Department of Mathematical Sciences, Michigan Technological University

Yellow Umbrella Books

an imprint of Capstone Press
Mankato, Minnesota

Let's Graph

This class is having a bake sale.
How can we keep track of how
much they sell? We can use
a graph!

A graph is a picture that helps us sort information. Graphs make things easier to understand and compare.

Bar Graph

A bar graph shows information in rows. We can compare the height or the length of the rows. Let's make a bar graph.

Two fruit pies have been sold at the bake sale. We can color in two bars on the graph.

Ten chocolate chip cookies
have been sold. We can color
in ten bars on the graph.

Six doughnuts have been sold. We can color in six bars on the graph.

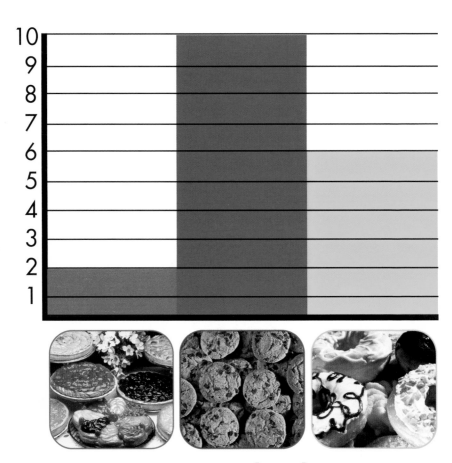

Let's compare the bars.
Which bar is the longest?
Which food has been sold
the most?

Which bar is the shortest?
Which food has been sold
the least? Graphs help us
compare.

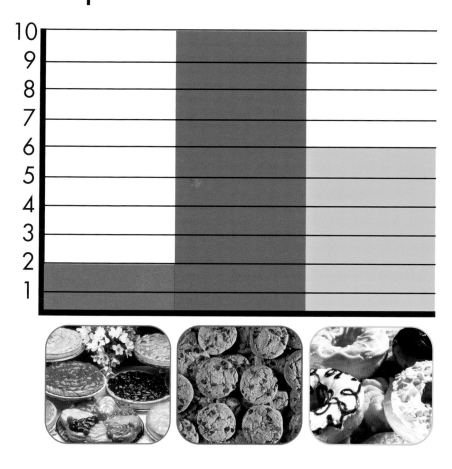

Pie Chart

A pie chart is a kind of graph.
A pie chart is a circle.
Let's make a pie chart.

The whole circle shows the total number of foods sold. The sections show how many were sold of each kind.

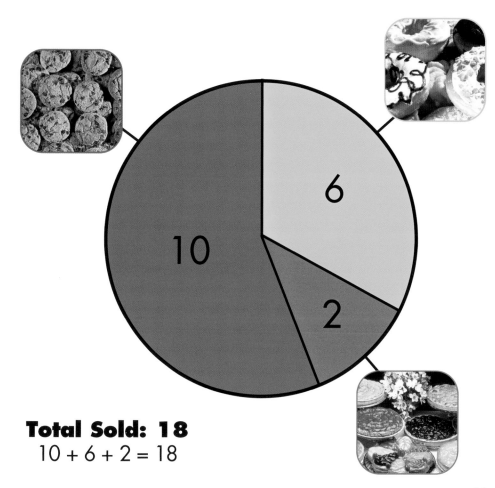

Total Sold: 18
10 + 6 + 2 = 18

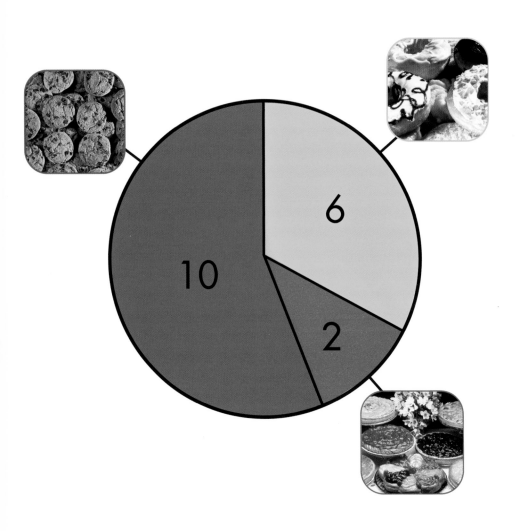

Which food was sold the most?
How can you tell?

Which food was sold the least? How can you tell?

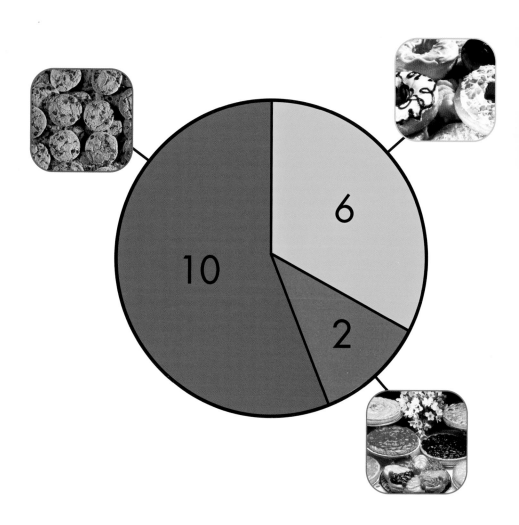

Learning from Graphs

The class will use the graphs to understand their sales. What will they learn?

Do you think they will bake more cookies or doughnuts next time?

Graphs help you count.
Graphs help you compare.
Let's graph!

Words to Know/Index

Word Count: 239
Early-Intervention Level: 15

Words to Know/Index

Word Count: 239
Early-Intervention Level: 15